COCAINE AND CRACK

What You Need to Know

Arnold M. Washton, Ph.D.
and
Donna Boundy, M.S.W.

ENSLOW PUBLISHERS, INC.

Bloy St. & Ramsey Ave.   P.O. Box 38
Box 777   Aldershot
Hillside, N.J. 07205   Hants GU12 6BP
U.S.A.   U.K.

Library of Congress Cataloging-in-Publication Data

Washton, Arnold M.
  Cocaine and crack.

  Bibliography: p.
  Includes index.
  Summary: Discusses facts about the effects of cocaine use, including the ease with which addiction can occur.
    1.   Cocaine habit—Prevention—Juvenile literature.   2.   Cocaine—Juvenile literature. 3.   Crack (Drug) —Juvenile literature.   [1. Cocaine habit. 2. Drug abuse] I. Boundy, Donna. II. Title.
HV5810.W27   1989   362.2'93   88–16814
ISBN 0–89490–162–1

Printed in the United States of America

10 9 8 7 6 5 4 3 2

Illustration Credits:
United States Coast Guard, p. 78; Reelizations, pp. 69, 75.

To my daughters, Tala and Danae, in the hope that their lives remain untouched by drugs.

—A.M.W.

To all young people striving to remain or become drug-free, in recognition of their courage.

—D.B.

Contents

1

An Epidemic of Cocaine Use

You've probably heard a lot about cocaine already. Maybe you've watched a cocaine bust on the evening news or read about a favorite athlete, movie star, or rock musician found with the drug. You may also have heard of the popular comedian who was badly burned trying to "freebase" cocaine or the college basketball star who died suddenly after sniffing cocaine with his friends.

But does all this add up to an "epidemic" of cocaine use? An epidemic is usually a fast-spreading disease. Can cocaine really cause a disease? Is its use, in fact, spreading?

Until recently, almost no scientific research had been done on cocaine. Even experts on drug abuse believed that cocaine, although illegal, was relatively harmless. Most of what was written about the drug said that it was mentally but not physically addictive.

Then drug abuse treatment programs all over the country began filling up with cocaine users who couldn't stop using the drug. It was ruining their health, affecting their families, and destroying their careers. For them, cocaine had indeed caused a "disease."

Experts began to study cocaine a little more closely. What they found was that far from being nonaddictive, cocaine may actually be the most addictive illegal drug of all. It just affects the body differently from some others such as heroin.

But this new knowledge about cocaine came too late for many people. Surveys show that 22 million Americans have already tried cocaine, and 5.8 million now use it regularly (at least monthly). An estimated 2 million are already addicted. By "addicted" we mean that they are unable to control their use, cannot stop when they try to, and are having problems in their lives as a result.

Even with these new facts about cocaine, many people are still trying it for the first time each day. No one can say for sure how many of these new users will eventually cross the invisible line from use to abuse and addiction, but experts predict a rate of about one out of every four.

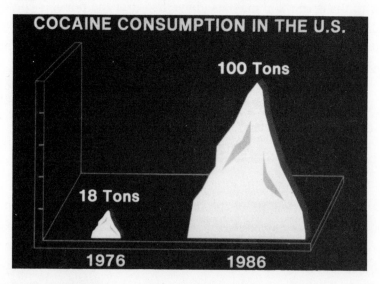

Cocaine consumption in the United States was five times greater in 1986 than in 1976 and continues to rise dramatically each year.

History Repeats Itself

You may be surprised to learn that this is not the first time cocaine has been popular in our country. Cocaine was used as a legal ingredient in many medicines during the late 1800s. It was considered something of a wonder drug then, thought to cure anything from nervous afflictions to headaches and depression.

Cocaine was also added to other products, including cigarettes, ointments, and even soft drinks. As you may have heard, Coca-Cola was so named because from the time it was first sold in 1886 until 1903, each bottle contained a small amount of cocaine!

The drug's popularity wasn't limited to America. A famous Viennese psychiatrist, Sigmund Freud, experimented with cocaine during the 1880s and initially hailed it as a cure for various forms of mental illness. Freud's hopes for cocaine were dashed, however, when the patients he prescribed it for eventually became addicted, as Freud himself is believed to have done.

By 1908 the view of cocaine as a miracle ingredient began to change here, also. Doctors began seeing patients who were unable to stop using it. Stories of cocaine addiction appeared often in newspapers, just as they do today. One article in *The New York Times* in 1908 referred to cocaine as "the most terrible vice ever acquired by a civilized people."

Concern spread throughout the country, and in 1914 the U.S. Congress passed its first drug abuse legislation, the Harrison Act. This new law made it illegal for cocaine to be used in any product. The first widespread cocaine epidemic began drawing to a close.

What's Different Now?

Today's epidemic of cocaine use is even more dangerous than the earlier one. For one thing, more people are using cocaine, and they are using it in greater amounts. At the peak of the nineteenth-century epidemic ten tons of cocaine were being used in various legal products each year. Today that much cocaine is sold on the street each *month!*

Second, the kinds of cocaine available today are much stronger in dose, not diluted in soda or cough syrup. Now, with the appearance of crack, a smokeable form of cocaine, there is even more to be concerned about. When smoked, cocaine reaches the brain in less than ten seconds, causing rapid and major changes in brain functioning. This means it carries even greater risk of medical and psychiatric emergencies, as well as bringing about quicker addiction. In fact, addiction to crack often occurs from within a few weeks or months of first trying it.

Finally, while the majority of cocaine users are adults, growing numbers of younger people are now becoming addicted, too. Because crack is sold in small quantities that seem cheap, more young people and people with low incomes try it. With crack's high addiction potential, many of these new users will become repeat customers.

Because teenagers are still growing, cocaine has an even more powerful effect on their internal organs, including the brain, than it does on adults'. So teens are even more likely to suffer medical or psychiatric damage from cocaine—or any other drug.

For the same reason, teenagers also become addicted more quickly. One survey found that teens who sniffed cocaine powder showed signs of addiction within 15 to 18 months of trying it, whereas adults averaged four years of use before reaching that point.

What Has Caused This Epidemic?

There are several reasons that cocaine use has become an epidemic now. For one thing, greater quantities of the drug are being produced than ever before. When the demand for cocaine in the United States began to rise in recent years, more South American farmers planted fields with coca, the plant from which cocaine is made.

Growing coca has become a chief source of income for many of these poor farmers. In fact, Bolivia exports more cocaine than it does any legal crop!

Because so much cocaine is being produced, the cost of the drug has dropped 50 percent in the past three years, also contributing to its wider use. Where a gram of cocaine (about a heaping teaspoonful) once cost $100 to $150, it now costs $60 to $80.

Federal drug enforcement officials are trying to stop the

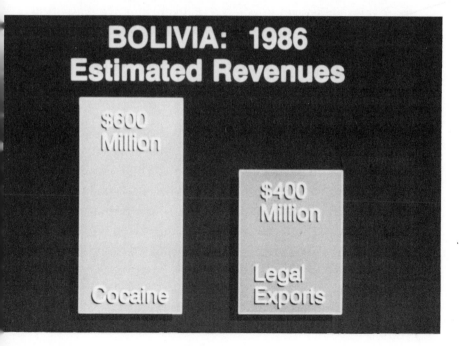

BOLIVIA: 1986
Estimated Revenues

$600 Million
Cocaine

$400 Million
Legal Exports

smuggling of cocaine into the United States, but with little success. Even though there are ten times more cocaine seizures and arrests being made now at our borders, seaports, and airports, the supply on the street is greater than ever before.

That's because smuggling and selling cocaine has become the most profitable business in the world, even though it is entirely illegal. The U.S. cocaine trade generated over $100 billion in profits in 1986. That's more than the profits made by any legal corporation!

But having cocaine available in larger supplies at lower prices still wouldn't result in widespread use if people didn't want to buy it. So another big reason for the current cocaine epidemic is the willingness of so many Americans to try it.

Beginning with the "drug culture" of the 1960s, attitudes toward illegal drug use in this country have grown more and more relaxed. Today, surveys show that one in five Americans over the age of twelve have used an illegal drug at least once during the previous year, and nearly one in ten have tried cocaine at some time in the past.

There are many reasons for this willingness to experiment with drugs like cocaine. People who believe that warnings about marijuana were exaggerated, for instance, often ignore warnings about cocaine, too. Others simply fall into the trap of thinking that addiction and other harmful effects won't happen to them. Young people in particular tend to ignore the future consequences of any risky or dangerous activity.

Finally, the effects of the cocaine "high" itself have played a big part in seducing so many people into trying it. People hear that cocaine makes you feel more confident, powerful, and energetic, and they want to get those effects. The fact that the high disappears in minutes and leaves the user feeling lower than before is often overlooked.

12

How Does All This Affect You?

The explosion of cocaine use over the past decade affects everyone in our society—even those who never try it themselves.

For one thing, police tell us that more cocaine means more crime in our neighborhoods. People addicted to a drug usually have to spend a lot of money for it. Sometimes out of desperation they turn to robbing people and homes. Addiction to crack in particular, police say, has caused a rise in some violent crimes, including murder.

The cocaine epidemic also costs us all money. With more workers using cocaine on their jobs, companies lose profits. Some of this loss is passed on to the public in the form of higher prices. In total, cocaine use is thought to cost Americans a whopping $49.6 billion each year!

But the cocaine epidemic has an even more direct and

The devastating effects of the cocaine epidemic, such as higher crime rates and health care costs, have been dramatically featured in the media.

tragic effect on the growing numbers of young people living with a parent who uses cocaine. Since approximately ten million Americans over age twenty-six used the drug in the past year, some 15 to 20 million children and teenagers may be affected.

This adult drug use is thought to be causing more births of drug-affected babies and higher rates of child neglect and abuse. It also means that many children are growing up with drug-using role models. Research has shown that such young people whose parents abuse alcohol or drugs are at increased risk of eventually becoming addicted to cocaine or other drugs themselves.

Finally, with more cocaine available at lower prices, there is simply a greater chance that you will be invited at some time to try it. And trying this drug means becoming one of the people at risk for getting hooked.

Getting addicted to or harmed by cocaine or crack has nothing to do with willpower, either. You can't will yourself not to become addicted. As long as you use the drug at all, you're taking a chance. Some of those now addicted to cocaine and crack didn't know this. If they had, they might have decided that it wasn't worth the risk.

2

Some Basic Facts

What Is Cocaine?

Cocaine is a powerfully addictive, illegal drug. The most commonly used form of it is cocaine powder, the chemical name for which is cocaine hydrochloride. Cocaine powder is white and odorless and is usually sniffed up the nose ("snorted"). It can also be dissolved in water and injected into a vein or changed into a form that can be smoked—such as crack.

All cocaine is imported from Central or South America. There it is extracted from the leaves of the coca plant, or *Erythroxylon coca*. These tall, waxy plants grow primarily in the Andean Mountain region.

Legally, cocaine is classified as a narcotic, along with drugs like heroin and opium. As such, it carries stiff penalties for possession or sale. But in the strict sense of the word, narcotics are drugs that dull the senses and cause drowsiness—which cocaine does not.

Chemically, cocaine is a local anesthetic, which means it numbs the body tissues it comes in contact with by blocking nerve conduction. This numbing action is not unlike that of the novocaine your dentist may use to numb your gums.

15

But unlike other anesthetics, cocaine also has a stimulating effect on the central nervous system similar to that of amphetamines, or "speed." Thus, when someone uses cocaine, the heart beats faster, blood is pumped quickly to all parts of the body, and the person feels more energetic as a result.

The stimulant effects of cocaine are what's known as the high, which lasts about twenty to thirty minutes when cocaine powder is snorted. For most people, the high is followed by an unpleasant "crash" during which they feel tired, depressed, and irritable and want to use more cocaine.

Both the high and the crash result from chemical changes cocaine causes in the brain. With repeated use, these chemical changes can cause addiction. Many other physical and emotional problems can result from using cocaine, too. It can even cause brain seizures or heart failure, and result in death.

Cocaine is extracted from the leaves of the coca plant, *Erythroxylon coca,* grown in the mountainous regions of Central and South America.

Such tragic reactions to cocaine, while not common, can occur without warning—even the first time it is used.

Before it is sold, cocaine is almost always mixed with other chemicals, some of them very dangerous. These other chemicals are called "cuts." They are added by the dealers in order to fill out the cocaine and make it weigh more. That way, the dealer can make more money with less cocaine.

The additives in cocaine are dangerous for two reasons. First, local anesthetics or amphetamines are often added by dealers because they cause physical effects (such as numbing or increased heart rate) similar to those of cocaine. This is done to fool the buyer into thinking the mixture contains more cocaine than it does. Also used as additives are drugs that raise blood pressure or change heart rhythms. All of these are powerful drugs themselves and can cause serious side effects.

Cocaine powder is usually mixed with other substances to make it weigh more before it is sold on the street. Some of these "cuts" are very dangerous.

Second, the user never knows for sure what has been added. Some dealers have been known to add whatever was handy, such as cornstarch, flour, or talcum powder. Even these substances, which you might not think of as dangerous, have caused blood clots in the lungs, resulting in death.

Cocaine is still used medically in surgery involving the eye, nose, and throat. In eye surgery, for example, it is used to numb the surface of the eye while the doctor performs the operation.

Except for these medical uses, the possession, manufacture and sale of cocaine are illegal in every state. Some people tend to overlook this, however, since many who break the drug laws are never arrested. But it is extremely important to remember that cocaine *is* illegal, because the penalties are very serious for those who are caught and convicted. In New York State, for instance, the minimum sentence for someone convicted of the criminal sale of cocaine is fifteen years to life.

What Is Crack?
Crack is a smokeable form of cocaine that is sold in tiny chunks or "rocks." It is an extremely dangerous drug that has caused the addiction of thousands of young people and adults since it first appeared for sale in Los Angeles in 1981. Crack is thought to get its name from the fact that it makes a crackling sound when heated.

Some users smoke crack in a special glass pipe that has water in the bottom of it. Others sprinkle crack into a marijuana joint or a regular cigarette and smoke it that way. Regardless of how it is smoked, the high from crack only lasts about five minutes.

Some young people have mistakenly assumed the because crack is smoked, it is not that dangerous to try. But the opposite is actually true. Crack has an immediate and very powerful effect on the user's brain—even more so than cocaine powder. Because of this powerful effect, it causes addiction very quickly, and is even more likely than other forms of cocaine to cause serious psychiatric and medical side effects. There are two reasons for this.

First, whenever a drug is taken into the lungs, it is immediately absorbed into the bloodstream and carried to the brain. Other routes take considerably longer. So while cocaine powder takes four to five minutes to reach the brain when it is snorted, crack arrives there in less than ten *seconds!*

The second reason crack has such a powerful effect on the brain is that it arrives at the brain in higher doses than through other methods of use. By the time cocaine powder travels through the body for four or five minutes, some of it has been absorbed by other tissues. Because crack moves so quickly to the brain, most of the dose taken arrives there.

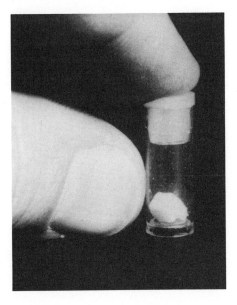

Crack, a smokeable form of cocaine, is sold in tiny chunks and usually packaged in vials. Crack causes rapid and severe addiction.

This fast delivery of high doses of cocaine to the brain is what causes both the high and the crash that follows it to be so intense. But it is also the reason that addiction to crack occurs more quickly than with other forms of cocaine. It is simply a scientific fact that high doses of an addictive drug delivered rapidly to the brain causes addiction to occur within a short period of time.

It may take only a few weeks of use for someone to become addicted to crack, and some people have reported being addicted from the very first time they used it. It is still important to remember, however, that addiction and all other dangerous consequences can result from using *either* cocaine powder or crack.

The idea of smoking cocaine is not a new one. Heavy cocaine users have been smoking a form of the drug for some time, and have called this freebasing. The term *freebase* means simply that the basic alkaloid, the cocaine base, has been freed through some chemical process from its hydro-

CRACK

- Smokeable Form of Cocaine
- Gets to the Brain in 8-10 Seconds
- Intense, Rapid "High"
- Lasts 3-5 Minutes
- Intense "Crash"
- Intense Cravings
- Rapid Addiction
- Severe Medical and
    Psychiatric Consequences

chloride salt. It is only in this freebase form that it can be heated easily enough to smoke.

Before crack was available, people who wanted to smoke cocaine had to convert cocaine powder into a smokeable form themselves. This was a very dangerous process, involving the use of ether, an explosive chemical. When comedian Richard Pryor accidently set himself on fire allegedly trying to do this, the public became more aware of this particular danger. Pryor survived, but was seriously burned over much of his body.

So what crack amounts to is a ready-made form of smokeable cocaine, or freebase. The dealers have already performed the chemical conversion process for the user.

Crack is usually sold in small plastic vials with colored stoppers. Each vial contains one to three rocks and costs from $3 to $20 or more. Crack may also be sold in small plastic bags or tubes, and there have been reports that it was sold in tablet form.

In some areas, crack is sold by "brand names," such as Super White, White Cloud, Cloud 9, and Serpico. Major centers of crack dealing are often located in inner-city neighborhoods, although people from all areas and walks of life go there to buy it.

Crack is sold openly on the street as well as in buildings known as crack houses. Crack houses are usually apartments that have been taken over by crack dealers. Users go there to both buy and use crack. Some of them stay for hours, or even a day or two, until all their money has been spent on the drug.

What Is Coca Paste?
Coca paste, known as "basuco" on the street, is probably the most dangerous of all forms of cocaine currently in use. Kerosene, leaded gasoline, and sulfuric acid are used in a sim-

ple process that extracts this pasty substance from the coca plant leaf. The paste is then dried and smoked in a pipe or cigarettes, much like crack.

The added danger of coca paste is that a lot of the kerosene and leaded gasoline used to make it remain in the paste and are taken into the lungs when smoked. In reality, it can cause severe lead poisoning for anyone who uses it. Many people have suffered permanent lung and brain damage as a result.

Because so little work goes into making coca paste, it is very cheap to buy. So far, it has been sold mostly in Bolivia and Colombia, where many people who try it are becoming quickly addicted. Recently, it has begun showing up on the streets of some U.S. cities.

3

Dangerous Myths

The cocaine epidemic has come about so suddenly and on such a wide scale that a lot of mistaken information is still being circulated. Here are some of the most common—and most dangerous—myths about cocaine and crack, followed by some very important facts.

> Myth: *"Cocaine is not physically addictive."*
> Fact: Cocaine may be the most powerful, physically addictive drug available on our streets today.

Most people think that if a drug is physically addictive, stopping it will result in severe physical symptoms, such as fever, nausea, and body aches. It is common to picture a heroin addict writhing in pain, trying to "kick the habit."

So when it was noted during the 1960s and 1970s that one could stop using cocaine and not get violently ill, many people—including experts on drug abuse—concluded that this drug was not physically addictive. Any urge to use cocaine repeatedly was seen as purely psychological.

Partly as a result of this myth, more and more people

were willing to experiment with cocaine who might not have been otherwise. Eventually, a large number found themselves unable to stop using the drug—no matter how much willpower they applied. So experts began looking more closely at cocaine's addictive powers.

What they learned is that addiction has little to do with whether a person goes through physical withdrawal symptoms or not. Addiction occurs when the user's brain chemistry has been altered to create a strong desire for more of the drug.

We know now that cocaine affects brain cell chemistry in such a way as to send faulty brain messages, making the person crave cocaine the same way a hungry person craves food. This is no less a physical addiction than that of the heroin junkie who writhes in pain waiting for the next fix.

The cocaine addict who tries to stop using the drug usually becomes very depressed and can't stop thinking about cocaine. It is not unusual for a regular user to break into a sweat just from hearing cocaine mentioned or to have dreams and nightmares about it.

These cravings may be even harder to endure than the flulike symptoms of heroin withdrawal. Most people who become addicted to cocaine, in fact, need help in order to stop.

> *Myth: "Sniffing a little cocaine is harmless."*
> Fact: Cocaine's harmful effects can result from *any* amount and method of use.

Many people still believe that if you snort "just a little" cocaine and don't smoke or inject it, you can't get addicted, suffer any serious medical harm, or die. All three of these assumptions are false.

Sniffing cocaine powder does *not* protect the user from addiction. In fact, the majority of those who become addicted have used it *only* in this way. The process is simply a little slower.

A person doesn't have to use cocaine every day in order to get addicted, either. Some people who become dependent on cocaine have used it only on weekends, or occasionally after work or school.

For someone with an underlying medical condition, "a little" cocaine can spell disaster. While death from sniffing cocaine is still not very common, when it does happen it is almost always unexpected and without warning.

Len Bias, a young college basketball star, died in 1986 from a cocaine-induced cardiac arrest, reportedly after celebrating his draft onto a pro team by sniffing cocaine with his friends. The doctor who examined his body after death said the amount of cocaine Bias had consumed would not necessarily be considered a high dose.

"This particular concentration might not kill another individual," said the medical examiner. "On the other hand, another individual could die at a lower level." So even a young, healthy person in good physical condition can die from a sudden, toxic reaction to cocaine—regardless of how it is used.

Yet some people do appear to use small amounts of the drug once in a while and show no *visible* signs of damaging effects or addiction. Even those people, however, are taking a big chance. Cocaine can affect the brain and other organs in slow steps, and damage may simply show up later.

Probably the biggest danger in using "a little" cocaine is that as one becomes tolerant to the drug, the brain starts to require more cocaine for the same high. Somewhere along the line, most users then start to increase the dose. Thus, a person using "a little" cocaine can cross the invisible line from use to abuse without even knowing it.

Myth: "Cocaine can help you do anything better."
Fact: In the long run, cocaine greatly increases
    your chances of failure.

Imagine there could be a magic way to change anything you don't like about yourself. If you are shy, this magic could transform you instantly into an outgoing, confident person who could easily talk to anyone. If you are tired or bored, suddenly you could become full of energy and interested in everything around you. With these new qualities, you could begin to feel more attractive to others.

Think how exciting it would be if these magical effects could last forever, and there was no price to pay for them. Sounds good, right? Unfortunately, that's what some people think they will get from using cocaine.

The truth is, cocaine only makes people feel they have these qualities for a very short time, during what's known as the "honeymoon" period of use, right in the beginning. After that, it produces exactly the opposite effects. But by then, the user may be on the way to addiction and unable to stop using the drug.

So instead of having more confidence and sociability, the steady cocaine user becomes depressed, irritable, paranoid, and sometimes even suicidal; instead of having more energy, he or she becomes tired and sickly; instead of becoming more attractive to others, the cocaine addict ends up appearing pale, drawn, and anything *but* attractive.

In short, the person who expects greater success after using cocaine usually ends up face to face with failure. Those who don't get help in time become unable to do much of anything well.

Unfortunately, though, the more desperately a person wants these short-term effects of cocaine, the more likely he or she is to become addicted. That's because a person who doesn't feel confident, attractive, or successful *without* cocaine is more likely to want to use the drug again and again to try and get that effect. Since repeated use makes addiction more likely, in time there is no more magic, but only a nightmare in which the person is trapped.

Some people think cocaine improves their sexual performance. In time, however, exactly the opposite is true of that too, and sexual interest decreases. Of the heavy cocaine users in one survey, 53 percent said they would rather use cocaine than have sex. Cocaine can also cause impotency, the inability to get an erection, in males.

Improved performance in sports is another effect some people have looked for in cocaine. A common experience described by athletes who try cocaine is that they have a good game after using it the first time and are lured into trying it again and again, hoping for a repeat performance. In almost every case, however, after a very short honeymoon period, cocaine use damaged performance instead. This brings us to another myth.

Myth: "Most successful athletes use cocaine."
Fact: Most successful athletes do *not* use cocaine or other drugs, and those who do are often not successful for long.

There is so much in the news about certain athletes who use cocaine or who are arrested on drug charges that it's easy to get the impression most successful athletes are on cocaine and other drugs. Some people then take that to mean, "So using drugs must not be that bad for you."

Both of these assumptions are false—and very misleading. The truth is, the vast majority of athletes with lasting success

27

are *not* using cocaine or other drugs. It only seems that way because we hear so much about those who are.

When someone down the street from you uses cocaine, chances are it doesn't make the national news. But when a famous athlete is discovered with this problem, it may very well make the front page. Because that person is well known already, what happens to him or her is considered news around the country.

Successful athletes do face a lot of pressure to use drugs, though. First, they too hear the myth that cocaine can improve performance and may be tempted to test it out. Second, people who want to rub elbows with sports celebrities often offer cocaine to them—free. And third, success in any field tends to make people forget that they are still vulnerable to addiction, arrest, and the other dangers of cocaine use.

For those athletes who do give in to cocaine use, it often spells the end of their success. Tim Raines, a Montreal Expos outfielder, tells one such story. During his first year in the major league, Raines set a league record for stolen bases by a rookie. Dazzled by success, the twenty-year-old decided to experiment with cocaine and by the following season was a daily user—and quickly becoming a loser.

"It certainly hurt my performance," Raines told a reporter after beginning treatment for his addiction. "I struck out a lot more, and my vision was lessened." Raines's batting average dropped twenty-seven points during the season when he was using cocaine, and he struck out nearly three times as often.

In a recent nationwide survey of 2000 college athletes, twelve percent reported using cocaine at some time in the past year, while 88 percent said they did not. A spokesman for the National Collegiate Athletic Association said these figures demonstrate that college athletes do not use cocaine more than others the same age.

The most recent results of another survey, this one by the National Institute on Drug Abuse, suggest he is right. Among all eighteen- to twenty-five-year-olds polled for that survey, 16.4 percent admitted using cocaine at some time in the past year. This is even higher than in the college athlete survey, though the higher age spread of eighteen to twenty-five may account for some of the difference.

Myth: *"Crack is a pure form of cocaine and there-fore safer."*

Fact: Crack is not pure at all but contains the same chemical cuts found in cocaine—in an even more dangerous form.

As you have learned, various chemicals, or cuts, are routinely put into cocaine powder by dealers to stretch it out and make it weigh more. Substances added as cuts range from cornstarch to local anesthetics and amphetamines (speed).

Many people falsely assume that these cuts are removed from cocaine when it is heated and made into crack. This is absolutely untrue. The cooking process that changes the powder into crack does *not* remove these chemicals; it simply concentrates them. So crack contains exactly the same substances that were in whatever cocaine powder it was made from—in an even more dangerous form.

When taken into the lungs through smoking, these concentrated additives go straight to the brain along with the cocaine. And because they reach the brain so quickly and in such potent form, they are even more likely to do damage than when sniffed in the drug's powdered form.

Myth: "Crack is cheap."
Fact: Crack is a very expensive drug. (Ask anyone
who has become addicted to it.)

Because crack is usually sold in tiny vials for as little as
$3, some people have come to see it as a cheap drug to use.
But crack only seems inexpensive because it is sold in such
small quantities. When equal weights of crack and cocaine
powder are compared, crack actually costs twice as much.

In addition to that, addiction occurs so fast with crack that
the user often ends up buying greater and greater amounts of
the drug, more and more often. The result is usually a very
expensive drug habit. Most crack addicts report spending between $100 and $200 each day on the drug. Few people would
consider that a bargain.

Myth: "The cocaine epidemic is a teenage problem."
Fact: The majority of cocaine and crack users in
this country are adults.

We often hear adults discussing ways to end the "teenage
drug abuse problem." It is true that illegal drug use among
American youth is higher than in any other industrialized nation in the world, and 17 percent of our high school seniors
have tried cocaine.

But it is a little-known fact that while cocaine use among
twelve- to seventeen-year-olds has nearly doubled in the past
ten years, use by people over the age of twenty-six has increased 7 times! Over 4 percent of both age groups now report using cocaine sometime in the past year.

When you add to this the fact that a whopping 16.4 percent of all eighteen- to twenty-five-year-olds used cocaine in

the previous year, it becomes clear that the cocaine problem is far from limited to high school teens!

In fact, until recently, cocaine use tended to *increase* with age, up to a certain point. There are a couple of reasons for this. First, cocaine was an expensive drug and adults were better able to afford it. This is changing somewhat now since crack is sold in small enough quantities to seem cheap and is accessible to teenagers.

Second, adults have been more likely to seek the kinds of performance-enhancing effects that cocaine provides in the beginning of use. Many adults who become trapped in addiction started using cocaine because they thought it was going to help them in their careers, by providing more energy and confidence.

A surprising number of teens now live in a home where a family member uses drugs. Those who don't can look around and see cocaine used on television and in the movies by favorite athletes and film stars. Probably for the first time in our history, in fact, we have a substantial number of adults "teaching" illegal drug use to the next generation.

4

A Powerful Addiction

Basic Brain Chemistry

You may be surprised to learn that your brain cells operate by chemical electricity, with certain chemical "transmitters" firing messages back and forth.

These chemical transmitters are called neurotransmitters because they transmit electrical charges from one nerve cell, or neuron, to the next. The electrical charges are actually tiny coded messages that tell the rest of your body and mind what to think and do.

Suppose right now you decided to reach out and pick up a pencil from the table in front of you. If we could look inside of your brain while you did that, we would see millions of tiny nerve cells firing chemical messages in certain parts of your brain.

The nerve cells that make up the pathway along which these messages travel don't actually touch each other. There is a tiny gap between each nerve cell, called the synapse. The neurotransmitters carry an electrical charge that fires across the synapse so that the coded messages in one nerve cell travel to the next one, and so on down the line.

The Brain's Reward Center

There are about twenty-five different types of neurotransmitters in the human brain. One of the most essential to mental activity is dopamine. It is also the neurotransmitter most affected by cocaine use.

Dopamine stimulates certain nerve cell circuits within what's known as the brain's reward center. The reward center is located in an area of the brain called the hypothalamus and provides you with pleasurable feelings whenever you satisfy one of your basic biological drives.

For example, when you are hungry and eat some food, your brain releases dopamine in the reward center. As the result of that dopamine release, you have feelings of satisfaction and pleasure. In this way, the basic drives for food, water, and sex are reinforced. We do these things over and over again—because it feels good!

These pleasure signals seem to be nature's way of making

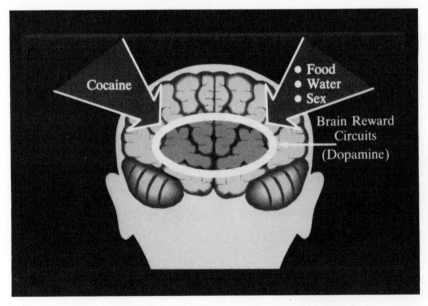

sure we continue to do the things essential to living. Let's look more closely at how these signals are sent.

In the reward center, dopamine is stored in microscopic storage areas, called vesicles, located on each nerve cell. Without any drug interference, the right amount of dopamine is naturally released from the vesicle as needed to help maintain a normal mood and mental state.

On each nerve cell there are also receptors to receive the dopamine that has jumped across the synapse from the previous nerve cell. Once the dopamine reaches the receptor, a special enzyme acts to neutralize it. That means the electrical message carried by the dopamine is extinguished, or put out. The receptor, therefore, gets the message, the dopamine is neutralized, and the message is not sent over and over.

Finally, any extra dopamine that has not been picked up by a receptor is carried back by a particular enzyme into the nerve cell that released it. This is called the reuptake process. There it is stored until it is needed for another release.

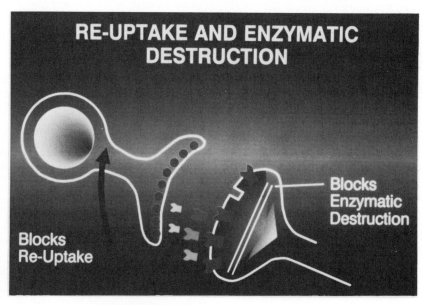

RE-UPTAKE AND ENZYMATIC DESTRUCTION

Blocks Enzymatic Destruction

Blocks Re-Uptake

Cocaine's Effect on Dopamine

When a person takes cocaine, all three parts of this basic process are affected. First, when the cocaine reaches the brain it causes the nerve cells to release a *flood* of dopamine, much more than it ordinarly would. This is what causes the rush of good feelings, or euphoria. It also causes the neuron to eventually run out of dopamine.

Second, cocaine destroys the enzyme that usually neutralizes the dopamine messages. So instead of getting the pleasure message for a limited period of time, the receptor keeps getting more and more of these neural impulses. The rush, or high, a person feels for a period of time occurs as long as these are still being fired.

Finally, cocaine also destroys the enzyme that carries extra dopamine back into the nerve cell that released it. In other words, it blocks the reuptake process, so the extra dopamine remains in the synapse, leaving the releasing nerve cell temporarily short on its supply.

The Cocaine Crash

The cocaine "crash" is caused by this temporary dopamine shortage. It takes time for the brain to make more dopamine. And since dopamine is essential to keep a normal mood and mental state, the dopamine shortage causes a crash.

A person in this state usually feels depressed, tired, and anxious; has trouble sleeping; and craves more cocaine. What the brain really needs is to rest and make more dopamine. But it has been chemically "misprogrammed" into craving more cocaine instead.

Beginning cocaine users who occasionally snort small amounts of the drug may not experience a crash, simply because their brain cells are not yet short of dopamine. With continued use and higher doses, however, this effect almost always occurs.

The crash is not unlike a hangover from alcohol. One or two drinks rarely result in a bad hangover, but five or six drinks very well might. The amount of cocaine it takes to cause a crash also varies from person to person.

A person who is crashing may try to escape the depression and restlessness by using other drugs. In one survey of teens calling a cocaine hotline, 92 percent reported using marijuana for this purpose, 85 percent used alcohol, and 65 percent used tranquilizers, sleeping pills, or some other "down." It's easy to see why cocaine addicts often end up addicted to other drugs as well.

Depression

With continued use of cocaine, the brain becomes over-worked, is unable to replace the lost dopamine, and becomes depleted. The depleted brain has been compared to a wet sponge that has been squeezed and squeezed until it no longer has any more liquid left in it.

Since dopamine is vital to maintaining a normal mood and mental state, a long-term deficiency of it can cause a person to become extremely depressed—to feel "low" almost all of the time. So instead of feeling energized by cocaine as in the early stages of use, the cocaine user at this stage feels tired, depressed, and unable to enjoy life.

The only thing that really helps a person with this condition is to stop taking cocaine, so that the brain can rest and recover. Unfortunately, though, most people in this state of cocaine-caused depression take more cocaine. That's because their brain messages are driving them to seek the drug over and over.

The cocaine user is then trapped in a vicious circle of craving the very drug that is causing the depression. This circle usually continues until a serious health, family, or financial crisis prompts the person to seek help out of desperation.

Without help, cocaine addicts who reach this state of depression have an abnormally high rate of suicide attempts, accidents, and overdoses.

Cravings for More Cocaine

Because cocaine stimulates the nerve circuits in the brain's reward center, repeated use of the drug causes the brain to react as if taking cocaine itself is necessary for survival.

That's why a user may begin to crave cocaine as if his life depended on it. In effect, a cocaine addict's brain cells have been short-circuited by the drug.

This explains why, for a regular user, getting and using cocaine begins to take priority over schoolwork, job demands, family responsibilities, and other interests. The brain has been fooled into reacting to cocaine as if it is necessary for survival, like food or water.

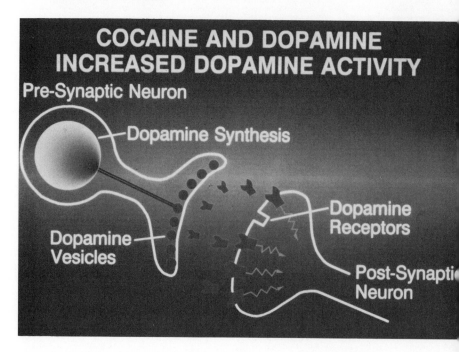

COCAINE AND DOPAMINE
INCREASED DOPAMINE ACTIVITY
Pre-Synaptic Neuron
Dopamine Synthesis
Dopamine Vesicles
Dopamine Receptors
Post-Synaptic Neuron

A number of laboratory experiments have demonstrated how cocaine can override even basic biological drives:

• Hungry monkeys given the choice of cocaine or food almost always choose cocaine and ultimately die of starvation or of reactions to the drug.

• Sex-deprived male monkeys will choose to press a bar for cocaine injections rather than mate with female monkeys placed in their cages.

• Animals allowed to have as much cocaine as they want will take such big doses that almost all will die of brain seizures within thirty days. The drive for cocaine seems to override even the basic instinct to survive!

In humans, this overriding of the basic drives results in serious health and social problems. Of the cocaine addicts in one survey, 59 percent reported a severe weight loss (due to not eating enough); 50 percent expressed a loss of interest in sex; 26 percent admitted stealing from employers, family, or friends in order to get money for cocaine; and 21 percent had turned to dealing drugs for the same reason.

Marriages break up, careers fail, and fortunes are lost on drugs while the cocaine addict goes after more cocaine.

Tolerance

Tolerance is the need to take more and more of a drug in order to get high. Scientists think that tolerance to cocaine develops because, with continued use, more receptors form on the nerve cells, requiring more dopamine to be released in order to fill them.

Eventually, a cocaine addict develops so much tolerance to the drug that he or she no longer even gets high from it. This person will still usually go on using cocaine, however, almost as if on automatic pilot. That's because the cravings continue to be stimulated by the brain's reward center, and because the crash is so uncomfortable.

At this point, the user may feel in a terrible bind. Taking cocaine is no longer pleasurable, but not taking it feels even worse. This is the point at which some will seek treatment. Others will increase their use even further in a desperate attempt to feel the pleasurable effects from cocaine again.

The Kindling Effect

While in time it takes more and more cocaine to get someone high, it apparently takes less and less to cause brain seizures. This is called reverse tolerance, or the kindling effect. It is so named because each use of cocaine can be compared to putting more kindling wood on a fire.

The causes of the kindling effect are still largely a mystery. All we know is that a regular cocaine user may take his usual dose of cocaine one day without a negative reaction, but the next time he uses that same dose it could be fatal.

Unfortunately, many cocaine users don't know about this effect. Because they need more and more cocaine to get high (due to tolerance), they often assume that they are becoming less sensitive to all of cocaine's effects. With each repeated use, however, they are growing more and more vulnerable to brain seizures.

5

Who Gets Addicted?

When most people think of a drug addict they picture somone who grew up in a ghetto, has little hope for the future, and turns to drugs as a way to escape the frustration of being trapped in poverty. Or they think of someone who is emotionally disturbed and trying to cope through drugs.

In either case, addiction is thought of as a weakness that some troubled people give in to. It is assumed to be a matter of willpower. "If they really wanted to stop using, they just would!"

A quick look at who gets addicted to cocaine, however, dispels these stereotypes, for the vast majority do not fit either of the above descriptions.

For one thing, until recently, most cocaine users came from families with at least average incomes. This was due in large part to the high cost of cocaine. Today it is much cheaper because of the surplus of cocaine available and the more affordable price of crack.

Generally speaking, many of those addicted to cocaine have also had at least an average amount of success at work or school before getting involved with the drug. The majority have no history of major psychiatric problems, and many have never abused other drugs.

All these facts illustrate that cocaine addiction can happen to anyone. Since addiction results from physical changes the drug causes in the brain, it does not matter what one's race, religion, sex, or nationality is. Cocaine has been called an "equal opportunity drug," for everyone has an equal opportunity of becoming addicted to it.

For some, addiction happens rapidly, after using crack just a few times. But many weekend users who snorted cocaine powder and thought they were not getting addicted have found themselves at some point no longer able to control their use.

One thing is known for sure. The more cocaine you use and the longer you use it, the greater your chances of getting addicted. And *anyone* will become addicted if he or she uses enough. Some people will simply get there on less cocaine or in a shorter time.

New studies show that people who grow up with a parent who is an alcoholic or drug abuser are at special risk for becoming addicted to cocaine if they experiment with it. No one knows for sure why this is so. It could be that a physical sensitivity to addiction is inherited and then activated by cocaine. Or it could be that a child simply learns to use drugs by copying a parent's behavior, or both.

Stages on the Road to Addiction
The road to addiction is not clearly marked. No one knows when he or she is moving from one stage into another, for the lines between are invisible. And for each person, the process may be a little different. The following stages can serve as guidelines, however, for understanding the addiction process:

Experimental use. When a person first tries cocaine and uses it a few times, he or she could be said to be an experimental user. The reasons people experiment with drugs vary, but it is often out of curiosity, because others are doing it, or to get a certain effect from it.

This first stage of cocaine use is sometimes called a "honeymoon period," because in this stage the user often feels no crash, no cravings for more, and sees no obvious harmful effects. Usually, at this point small amounts of the drug are consumed, and the use is infrequent. (People who smoke cocaine, such as crack users, often skip this first stage altogether.)

During this honeymoon period, users also tend to experience many of the pleasurable effects of cocaine. They may feel energized by it, euphoric, self-confident, talkative, and sexually stimulated. A person at this stage can mistakenly conclude that cocaine use is both beneficial and harmless.

Unfortunately, experimenters who continue to use cocaine run a very high risk of moving into the next stage. Not

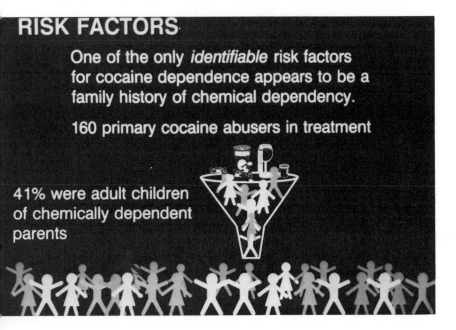

RISK FACTORS

One of the only *identifiable* risk factors for cocaine dependence appears to be a family history of chemical dependency.

160 primary cocaine abusers in treatment

41% were adult children of chemically dependent parents

everyone who tries cocaine will do so, of course. Some people stop here and never use it again. But it is true that everyone who became a regular user or addict started out as an experimental user.

Regular use. In this stage, using cocaine starts to become a regular part of the person's lifestyle. This person may use cocaine every time there's something important to do, or every weekend, or at every party. It begins to be hard to think of doing certain things or of having a good time without cocaine.

People sometimes refer to this as recreational use. People at this stage often still have not begun to suffer any obvious bad effects, so they too may conclude that cocaine is harmless for them.

This is actually a very dangerous stage because the biochemical changes, such as the dopamine depletion and the stimulation of the reward center, are taking place in the brain. The regular user may be crossing that invisible line into addiction without even realizing it.

Addictive use. In this stage the person no longer has control over cocaine but is controlled by it. At this point, dopamine depletion has taken place in the brain. The person has developed tolerance to cocaine and keeps increasing the dose. There are several outward signs that addiction has taken place.

First, the addicted user is preoccupied with getting and using cocaine. It becomes more of a priority than almost all other activities, even though he or she may no longer be getting high from it.

Second, the addict cannot control the amount of cocaine used. Whatever cocaine is available at any one time will be used up—often in binges lasting a whole day or more.

Third, the addict continues to use the drug despite negative consequences that begin to happen: medical problems; depression; paranoia; suicidal feelings; loss of job, money, or relationships; legal problems; and so on.

Finally, the cocaine addict usually denies or downplays the bad effects cocaine is having, denies that there is a problem, and gets angry if someone else suggests there is.

A Special Note About Crack Addiction

The high dose of cocaine in crack reaches the brain quickly because it is taken in through the lungs. This causes dopamine levels to rise quickly and dramatically, resulting in the intense high crack users describe.

The acute shortage of dopamine that follows causes an intense and miserable crash. It is this radical rise and fall of dopamine levels that causes crack's more rapid addiction. The process is simply sped up.

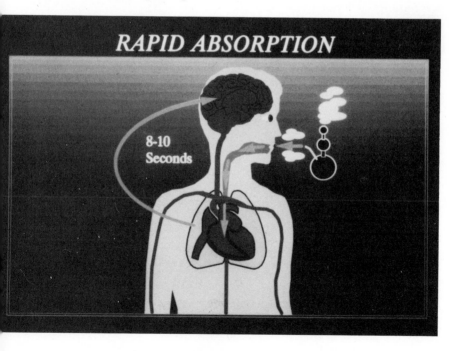

RAPID ABSORPTION

8-10 Seconds

6

Cocaine's Other Risks

Predictable Effects

Beyond addiction, there are other physiological effects—
some quite harmful—that predictably occur from using cocaine. People often think that *they* will be able to use the drug
and avoid these effects somehow. But that's like thinking one
can eat a big slice of cake and not take in a single calorie. It is
physically impossible!

The truth is, certain things happen in the heart, bloodstream, brain, and other organs—every single time cocaine is
used. It doesn't matter how smart you are, how experienced
you are at using drugs, or how determined you are to avoid
problems with cocaine. These effects occur in every user,
every time.

Let's focus for a moment on Julie, a fictitious twenty-year-
old college student. Suppose Julie has never used cocaine before but decides she's going to try it with some friends. Here's
what would happen inside her body with this first—and every
following—dose of cocaine she takes.

Nose is irritated. Assuming that Julie sniffs the cocaine,
we know that the drug will irritate the lining of her nose. To

47

help soothe the irritation, her body will automatically produce extra mucus, or fluids, in her nose, causing it to run.

If Julie keeps using cocaine, this continued irritation may cause a break or hole in the partition between her nostrils. The chemicals in cocaine can eat away at the tissues until they dissolve.

Lungs are damaged. If, instead, Julie smokes the cocaine, her entire respiratory system—including her throat and lungs—will become irritated. As with any kind of smoking, this occurs in part because the hot smoke is inhaled. Julie may cough, get a sore throat, or have chest congestion.

But the chemicals in cocaine will also damage the cells of her lungs. If she continues to smoke it, it will eventually damage those lung cells so much that they will be unable to perform their basic function of taking in oxygen and removing carbon dioxide from the bloodstream.

This lung damage begins the first time Julie uses cocaine, although it may not result in a loss of lung function until after much use. As this damage begins to become evident, she may experience shortness of breath and a constant cough.

Brain activity is altered. However Julie uses the cocaine, it will next go to her brain. In addition to affecting the reward center there, cocaine will alter other brain activity, too, including the thinking processes. Julie may have trouble concentrating and find herself losing memory.

Cocaine will also alter the area of Julie's brain that controls judgment. Situations in which she would ordinarily be cautious might now appear safe to her. She may feel trusting and warm toward the people around her when she is high—even when that trust is not deserved.

In this vulnerable state, someone like Julie is more likely to take dangerous risks and give in to pressure from others. This altered judgment could cause Julie to do things she later regrets or result in her being harmed by people she has trusted.

Central nervous system speeds up. Every time Julie uses cocaine it will also affect the part of her brain that controls metabolism. All internal bodily functions are sped up, something like changing the speed on a record player from 33 to 45 rpm.

It will increase the speed at which her heart beats and will make it pump more forcefully, placing a major strain on this most vital organ. This increased heart pumping causes more blood to be carried to all parts of the body, resulting in a sense of increased energy.

Many people, however, feel an excess of energy, more than they can use up. The result is a feeling of restlessness. About 75 percent of cocaine users say they cannot get to sleep when they want to. This condition is called insomnia. Insomnia, combined with an overworked central nervous system, causes most regular cocaine users to become chronically tired.

The extra blood pumped to Julie's brain may also cause her to feel overalert. For some people that brings about feelings of anxiety, fear, suspicion, and irritability.

Blood pressure rises. Cocaine is a powerful vasoconstrictor. That means it will cause Julie's arteries and veins to narrow. So while her heart is pumping faster, her blood vessels will hold less blood. This causes the blood to exert great pressure against the walls of the arteries, producing an increase in blood pressure.

This increased blood pressure occurs every time Julie uses cocaine, and it is one of the most dangerous effects, as you will learn in the next section.

Cocaine-Caused Emergencies

Up to this point, we've been talking primarily about the predictable, common effects that anyone can expect to have happen from using cocaine. There are also toxic reactions—medical or psychiatric emergencies—that *sometimes* occur.

These are totally unpredictable. Some people use cocaine over a long period of time and never have a toxic reaction. Other people use it without a problem for a while, then one day suffer a brain seizure. A small number of people have a severe or fatal reaction to cocaine the very first time they use it.

Because cocaine use has increased dramatically in recent years, the number of toxic reactions reported has increased, too. In 1982 there were approximately 4,000 admissions to hospital emergency rooms due to cocaine. Just three years later, that figure had more than doubled to 10,000. Here are some common causes:

Panic attacks. By altering brain activity, cocaine can prompt a sudden state of extreme anxiety and fear, known as an anxiety or panic attack. This is one of the most common reasons for cocaine-caused emergency room visits.

A person having a panic attack often feels frightened of losing his or her mind, or of having a heart attack and dying. Fortunately, a panic attack is usually short, subsiding as the drug effects wear off.

Someone having a panic attack needs to be kept in a quiet place and given calm reassurance that it will pass. Without such help, a person in this state of confusion and terror may be capable of extreme behavior, including suicide.

Cocaine psychosis. A small number of people have a sudden "psychotic break" from using cocaine. Others develop cocaine psychosis over a period of heavy use. Cocaine-related emergency room visits are caused by both types.

To be psychotic means to be out of touch with reality at least to some degree. A psychotic person may hallucinate (hear voices or see things that aren't really there) or become delusional (thinking or believing things that aren't true).

Victims of cocaine-induced psychosis often have paranoid delusions, in which they fear that someone is "after them." Let's look for a moment at one example.

Jack, twenty-six years old, sits at the attic window of his house. Sandbags are piled up nearby, ready to be thrown into place. An old .22 rifle stands against the windowsill. Jack will sit there all day and well into the night, hardly moving even to eat.

Jack has been smoking cocaine daily for the past year. Before that he snorted cocaine, on and off, for four years. The thought patterns in his brain have been gradually affected by the drug to the point where he is now suffering from cocaine psychosis.

He believes that people are after him and want to kill him. He is obsessed with this fear. Jack also hears cars in the driveway that aren't there, and footsteps coming up the attic stairs at night. Once he saw a pile of snakes winding around his bedpost.

There are many similarities between Jack's psychosis and the kind caused by a mental illness such as schizophrenia. Cocaine psychosis is actually self-induced mental illness. By using cocaine at high doses over a long period of time, a person is in effect choosing to become mentally disturbed.

The only good news here is that cocaine psychosis is often temporary. If Jack gets help and stops using cocaine, there is a very good chance his psychosis will clear up. Sometimes, however, the drug brings out other underlying psychiatric problems that the person didn't know were there. In that case, stopping the drug may not clear up the psychosis.

The very fact that people can become mentally ill from using cocaine is pretty dramatic evidence that the drug *is* affecting brain chemistry!

Brain seizures. Another common but very serious toxic reaction to cocaine is brain seizures. These occur when cocaine's affect on nerve cells in certain areas of the brain cause it to go into a state of "overload." When this happens, the electrical messages normally sent from the brain to the muscles, respiratory system, and heart and other organs can become chaotic and faulty.

The result can be epileptic-like convulsions, or muscle jerks and twitches; loss of motor control; and even loss of consciousness. When having seizures, it is not unusual to urinate or have a bowel movement, because control of all body functions and muscles is temporarily lost. About 19 percent of callers to a cocaine hotline reported brain seizures resulting in these symptoms.

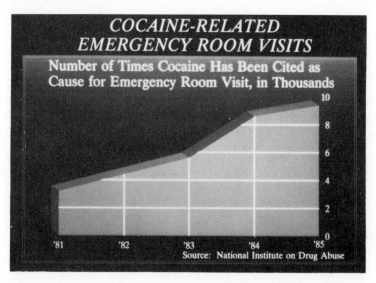

Cocaine-related emergency room visits more than doubled from 1981 to 1985. By 1987 they had more than doubled again to 24,000 visits per year.

But brain seizures can be even more serious than that. When they interrupt signals to the lungs or heart, these organs may simply stop working. Known as respiratory failure and cardiac failure, these are among the most common causes of cocaine-related death.

The amount of cocaine it takes to cause brain seizures cannot be predicted. It is known, however, that with each use the risk increases, due to what is known as the kindling effect. Some people lack the chemical that breaks down cocaine in the body, and can have seizures and die from cocaine the very first time it is used.

Heart attack. As you've learned, cocaine increases blood pressure every time it is used. In some cases, blood flow to the heart muscle is severely reduced or cut off by the narrowing arteries, and heart muscle begins to die. This is a heart attack.

People with any form of heart disease are in particular danger using cocaine. An irregular heartbeat that ordinarily causes no problem, for example, might become wildly erratic with cocaine use and stop the heart from pumping blood to the vital organs, including its own heart muscle. Unfortunately, many people with minor kinds of heart disease are not even aware that they have it.

Stroke. Cocaine also causes blood vessels leading to the brain to narrow, exerting pressure against the blood vessel walls. If the pressure becomes great enough, this can cause a vein or artery to burst, known as a brain hemorrhage.

The resulting leakage of blood in the brain damages brain tissue, leading to symptoms that are called a stroke. *Stroke* is the common term for a sudden paralysis or loss of sensation resulting from damaged brain tissue.

Cocaine can also cause a stroke by so limiting blood flow to the brain that tissue there is damaged by a lack of oxygen.

Death From Cocaine

About 600 people die each year in this country from cocaine, according to official statistics. This is a small figure compared to the large number who try the drug. Some experts believe, however, that there are many more such deaths than are officially reported.

There is another reason to be concerned, too: Death by cocaine cannot be predicted. However rare, it has occurred among both regular and first-time users, and from both small and high doses. Here are some of the factors contributing to cocaine-related drugs.

Overdose. When a person has a serious toxic reaction from cocaine, the dose taken could be called an overdose. An overdose is not, however, always a large dose. What is considered a small dose for one person may be an overdose for another. Even the same person may react differently to the same dose of cocaine on two separate occasions!

When a cocaine user takes what turns out to be an overdose, a number of things occur in the body that can lead to death. One of the most common is respiratory failure. Initially, a high dose of cocaine speeds up breathing, due to stimulation of the metabolism. But this control center in the brain can be overtaxed by such stimulation and produce a brain seizure.

When that happens, the electrical messages sent to the lungs and respiratory system can be thrown into chaos, causing the person to become unconscious and stop breathing. In effect, he or she has suffocated.

Fatal cardiac arrest can also result from an overdose. This occurs when the overstimulation of the brain sends faulty electrical messages to the heart, which then stops. In a small number of cases, high doses have actually numbed or "frozen" part of the heart muscle, making the heart unable to pump normally.

There are several ways a person increases the risk of overdosing. One is binge use, where an extremely high amount of the drug is used over a continuous period of time. Another is by smoking freebase or crack, which delivers high, concentrated doses to the brain quickly. A third way is by using unusually pure or "good" cocaine, which the dealer has not cut much.

Heavy cocaine users circulate several myths about how to help someone having an overdose reaction. Some say getting the person into a cold shower will help. Others suggest injecting a milk solution, or heroin, or barbiturates. All of these home remedies, however, are useless, and injecting *anything* is downright dangerous.

Dangerous drug combinations. You may remember that a famous actor and comedian, John Belushi, died a few years ago from a combination of heroin and cocaine, commonly called a speedball.

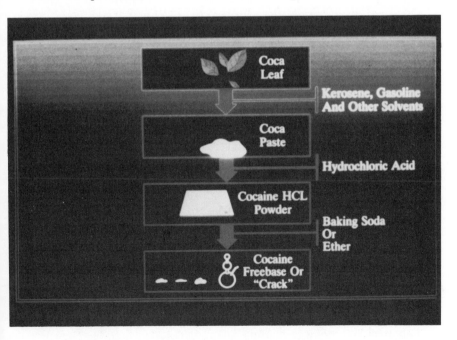

Belushi, most famous for his parts on the television show "Saturday Night Live" and the movie *Animal House,* reportedly had used cocaine many times before—with and without heroin. But for whatever reason on the night he died (perhaps the size of the doses, his condition, or the drug's purity) the combination proved fatal.

Combining cocaine and heroin is especially dangerous because both drugs at certain dosage levels slow down breathing. Together, they can cause a person to stop breathing altogether. In addition, this combination increases the likelihood of brain seizures.

Cocaine-related auto accidents. Over 15 percent of the teenagers who called a cocaine hotline had already been involved in a cocaine-related auto accident. Police suspect the true numbers are even higher. Few states test for drugs at the scene of accidents, so most cocaine-related crashes go unnoted.

The combination of cocaine and alcohol is especially dangerous behind the wheel. Because cocaine makes a person feel alert and in control, it can mask the depressant effects of alcohol. Someone high on both drugs can appear and feel alert, wide awake, and capable of driving—for a short time.

When the cocaine wears off about thirty minutes later, however, this same person may suddenly show all the signs of being drunk and unfit to drive. The effects of the alcohol suddenly take over, and the driver can even fall unconscious at the wheel.

Injecting cocaine and the risk of AIDS. A small number of cocaine users (less than 5 percent) use a needle to inject a cocaine-and-water solution directly into their veins. This is extremely dangerous today for several reasons.

For one thing, injecting a drug greatly increases the chances of a toxic reaction. That's because it delivers the drug quickly to the brain in a highly concentrated form, much as smoking it does.

But an even more serious danger today is the possibility of contracting the virus causing Acquired Immune Deficiency Syndrome (AIDS), a fatal disease, through use of an infected needle.

People who inject drugs often share needles because they are illegal to buy in most states. Since many people infected with the AIDS virus do not yet know they have it, it is frequently passed on to other drug users this way.

The number of intravenous (IV) drug users who are carriers of AIDS is now tragically—and dangerously—high. In New York City, where there are more IV drug users than anywhere in the country, a full 50 percent are thought to be infected. It is easy to see that sharing a needle today is nothing short of suicide.

"Cocaine Babies"

Doctors warn that there is no such thing as safe, "recreational" use of cocaine—*even once*—during pregnancy. Any drug a pregnant woman takes is delivered through her bloodstream to the unborn baby and goes to the baby's developing brain. But because a fetus is so tiny, the impact of even a small amount of cocaine can be very powerful.

Let's trace the different kinds of damage cocaine can do during pregnancy. First, there is the effect upon the term of the pregnancy itself. In one study, 38 percent of those who used cocaine while pregnant had a miscarriage. That means the woman's body expelled the developing fetus very early, ending the pregnancy. In general, only about 10 percent of all pregnancies end in miscarriage.

Among pregnant cocaine users who don't have a miscarriage, an abnormally high number go into early labor, before their babies are entirely formed.

Using cocaine also places the mother herself at higher risk of having a stroke as the result of brain hermorrhage or reduced blood flow to the brain. That's because cocaine places a heavy strain on the user's heart and blood pressure, which are both already under strain during a pregnancy.

Most tragic of all is the damage done to the developing fetus, which has no choice in the matter. Yet many pregnant women don't discover they are pregnant for at least several weeks. During that time, *any* amount of cocaine used could already have damaged the baby.

Let's assume that Julie, whom we met at the start of this chapter, has now graduated from college and gotten married. She and her husband, Bob, both consider themselves "social" cocaine users.

Only at special events do they indulge, and they see nothing wrong with that. After all, they say, they don't drink like some other people they know. And they don't see themselves turning into "junkies."

On Julie and Bob's first wedding anniversary they have a small party with close friends. One of their friends brings the cocaine, and after dinner they all sit around and get high. Because it's a special day, Julie takes more cocaine than she usually would.

Three weeks later, Julie discovers she is pregnant. What she doesn't know—and won't find out until the birth—is that her baby suffered irreversible brain damage from the cocaine Julie took that one night. Christy is born paralyzed on one side.

Because cocaine made Julie's blood pressure rise, it caused pressure to rise in the tiny blood vessels of the baby's brain and one of them burst. This in turn caused a stroke by damaging brain tissue. Christy is left with permanent physical and mental handicaps.

Many other cocaine-affected babies begin life in withdrawal from the drug for the first two to three weeks of life. These infants typically suffer high rates of respiratory and kidney disease, visual problems, lack of coordination, and developmental retardation. They are also thought to be at higher risk for crib death, the sudden unexplainable death of a baby during sleep.

With the higher incidence of premature delivery, cocaine babies are often born underweight as well. Typically, such babies are more cranky than others and have trouble sleeping. As toddlers, they may continue to be irritable and develop behavior problems.

The effects of smoking cocaine freebase or crack on a pregnancy are even more severe. Almost half of all babies born to crack users at one New York hospital showed signs of nerve disorders. This showed up in irritability, muscle stiffness, and tremors.

After delivery, if a nursing mother uses cocaine, it will be passed to the baby through her breast milk.

Other Uncalculated Risks

Behavior and values change. Nathan is a sixteen-year-old boy who started using crack recently. A star basketball player at his high school, he had always been out-going, funny, and fairly popular with other students.

Nathan first smoked crack at a party during his junior year. He only expected to try it once, but within six weeks he was using it every day. Soon Nathan's personality began to change. Instead of smiling and clowning, he became depressed, irritable, and short-tempered. His friends said he was "jumping down people's throats" over the littlest things.

Nathan withdrew from his circle of friends, staying more and more by himself. Needless to say, his behavior started to cause problems on the basketball court, where team spirit is so important. That, combined with missing practices and even a game once, got him thrown off the team eventually.

After that, Nathan grew even more isolated. Money started disappearing from the cash register at his part-time job and from his mother's pocketbook. It took a while for people to suspect Nathan of stealing. He had never done anything like that before.

The most frightening change to see in Nathan, according to his family and friends, was his temper. Where Nathan had once been easy-going and light-hearted, since using crack he always seemed "ready to fight." He even punched his best friend, accusing the friend of trying to "rip him off." The friend had merely asked to borrow a tape, something they had exchanged with each other many times before.

But Nathan was growing paranoid—suspicious and fearful that people were out to get him. In crack and other cocaine users, such paranoid feelings very often contribute to violent behavior. In fact, Nathan's story illustrates many of the ways in which cocaine can affect a person's personality, behavior, and values.

Many who become addicted to cocaine turn to stealing, as Nathan did, or to dealing drugs and other illegal activities in order to get money for cocaine. It is also common to sell jewelry, clothing, the family television set, anything within reach, to raise money for the drug. Exchanging sex for drugs is common too.

In most cases, these are things that the person would not have done before becoming addicted. Those who stop cocaine and get help often feel a lot of regret and embarrassment about the things they "stooped to" while addicted.

But these behavior changes are actually part of the addictive disease. That is, they are the result of changes the drug has caused in brain functioning. What happens is that the cravings for cocaine, caused by the altered brain chemistry, make getting and using cocaine seem more important to the user than anything else.

Often, people who do illegal or hurtful things while addicted to cocaine or crack report that they did not even feel any guilt at the time. The behavior is out of their control, in a sense, because the changes in the brain's chemical messages cause them to seek cocaine just the way a starving person would seek food. It's almost as if they have been "mis-programmed."

Needless to say, seeking cocaine above all else leads addicted users into many other problems. Most often, the user ends up heavily in debt, having sold everything of value. There may be arrests or other legal problems. Often failures at work and school result from being preoccupied with drug activities.

Violent behavior is often brought out too, even if that person never acted violently before. Among crack users who called a cocaine hotline, in fact, 38 percent reported this cocaine-caused behavior change.

Police say there has been a steady increase in violent crime associated with cocaine and crack use. One of many tragic examples of this occurred recently when a sixteen-year-old crack addict stabbed his mother to death when she found him smoking the drug.

The biggest toll in terms of human suffering may be the effect all of these behavior changes have on the family of the user. The chronic user often withdraws from his or her family, preferring to be alone or with other drug users. If the user is a parent, it is common for the children to be neglected. Even small children are left home alone for hours, even days, while addicted parents seek and use cocaine or crack.

In New York City alone, there has been a 30 percent rise in reports of neglected and abused children recently. Authorities attribute this largely to crack-using parents. There are also scores of babies in most major cities left behind in hospitals after birth because addicted parents are unable or unwilling to care for them. These babies are often born addicted and suffer various kinds of physical and mental damage from the cocaine received in the womb.

Effects on concentration and memory. Various kinds of damage to mental functioning can occur over a period of cocaine use, some of which have already been discussed. Though rarely mentioned, it is becoming apparent that the part of the brain that controls concentration and memory may also be affected by using cocaine. In one study of teen callers to a cocaine hotline, in fact, 65 percent said they suffered from "poor concentration" and 63 percent from "memory problems" since they started using cocaine.

Physical appearance affected. One of the main reasons people try cocaine is that they think it will make them more socially desirable. They enjoy some of the early effects of cocaine, like feeling more talkative, more confident, able to initiate conversations. They may even feel more sexual desire in the beginning.

But it is another one of the drug's contradictions that with continued use most people end up feeling and looking anything *but* physically and sexually attractive.

For one thing, most heavy cocaine users lose a lot of weight, because getting and using cocaine even takes priority over eating meals. This kind of weight loss, however, is almost never attractive. Most chronic users also look "washed out" and pale, their skin sunken-in around the eyes and other prominent bone structure. Poor nutrition and even malnutrition may result too.

Also, getting and using cocaine or crack becomes so important that the user no longer cares about appearance. Most heavy users stop putting any time or effort into grooming or hygiene, buying or cleaning clothes, or getting health care. The result is usually a severely neglected, even "derelict" kind of look—and that doesn't help anyone's appearance of self-confidence.

"You just feel ugly," is how one high school boy, Jerry, put it. Jerry lost forty pounds while using crack over a six-month period. "You don't want to look in the mirror because you know you look disgusting.

"You feel your face and your face is sunken in. You look at your stomach and your ribs are sticking out. I really hated the way I looked. I looked like I was worth nothing, and I *felt* like I was worth nothing."

7

If Someone You Care About Has a Cocaine Problem

Eric, now fifteen, can remember a time before cocaine became a problem in his home. Those days seem like something of a dream now. He remembers fishing with his dad, Sunday afternoon bike rides, and even a family vacation to Disneyland. Sometimes they would argue a little, like every family he knew, but not for long—and never over anything important.

But when Eric was eight years old, the problems began. His father, the owner of a small but successful business, began coming home from work later and later. Some weekends he wouldn't show up at all. When he was home, he and Eric's mother did nothing but fight about his absences.

Eric didn't know then that cocaine was at the root of the problem. What he did know was that his father's personality changed a lot. He would seem sullen and irritable one minute, then talkative and affectionate the next. Eric never knew what to expect.

Once, when some of Eric's friends were there, his father started acting strange, locking himself in the bathroom and accusing Eric and his mother of being against him. Eric was so

65

upset and embarrassed in front of his friends that he promised himself never to bring friends home again. He kept his promise, too.

Things continued to get worse. At one point, they had to move out of their home practically overnight when Eric's father sold it. Now Eric realizes that the money went to buy drugs. Later on, he sold the business, too. There were more horrible arguments between Eric's parents.

A few times the arguments grew violent, like the time his father shoved his mother hard against the wall and threatened to hit her. Nothing like that had ever happened before. The cocaine was profoundly affecting his father's judgment and values. He didn't even seem like the same person anymore.

By this time, Eric had heard cocaine mentioned enough in the arguments to know that this was a big part of the problem. Then he and his mother had a heart-to-heart talk about it, which helped clear up a lot of the confusion.

Eric's father did eventually get help, but only after the police came and arrested him. This once successful businessman had gotten so desperate for money to buy cocaine that he had taken part in some illegal business dealings.

The judge in his case, who was apparently knowledgeable about drug problems, allowed Eric's father to enter a cocaine treatment program rather than go to jail. Eric and his mother also got help so they could begin to get their own lives back on the track again, too.

When Is It a Problem?
Since 5 million American adults now use cocaine regularly, a large number of young people live with a parent or other relative who uses the drug. Not every family suffers such obvious and dramatic problems as Eric's. Another parent might use cocaine occasionally for many years without any apparent difficulty.

Sometimes, a family drug abuse problem is simply denied. That is, family members don't acknowledge or talk about it—with themselves or others. Children in this case get the unspoken message that the drug use is something to be ashamed of and hidden from outsiders. The result can be intense feelings of isolation and confusion.

How can you know if someone else's cocaine use is a problem? It has been said that if it interferes with the user's health, relationships, or ability to make a living, then it is a problem. Using those criteria, few would argue that Eric's father was in trouble.

But what about the user who seems to function OK at work, at school, and in relationships and who remains in seeming good health? Can we say for sure that such a person does *not* have a drug problem? The answer is *no!*

Because of the gradual changes cocaine causes in brain chemistry, *any* use of this drug may cause a problem. That's because a little use of cocaine encourages more use, and each time pushes the person a little closer to both addiction and other physical and mental health problems.

But there is still another way to look at the question. Suppose you worry about someone else's cocaine use—so much that you can hardly concentrate on your own life. In your efforts to get that person to stop, you become frustrated, hurt, and angry.

If that person's drug use is affecting you in any way—your moods, your functioning, your self-esteem—*you* now have a problem. Your problem is how to cope with the effects that the drug use has on you. The truth is, we can never force another person to see things our way and get help. But changing how we react to their drug use is something we *can* do.

What You Can (and Can't) Do

About a year after Janine and her boyfriend, Matt, started

going out together, he started using cocaine. Within a few months, that was all he cared about. Matt started spending more time with his drug-using friends and less with Janine. He even cut school sometimes to get high.

Janine kept wondering what she could do to get Matt to stop, to show him that being with her was better than using cocaine. She bought new clothes with her babysitting money, tried new hairdos, and was as bubbly and interesting as she could be around him. But Matt kept using cocaine.

Then Janine tried another approach. She told him she loved him and cried and begged him to stop using drugs. She asked him to do it for her, if nothing else. Matt agreed to try, and he actually did stop for a couple of weeks. Then it started all over again.

Janine's mother, concerned about Matt's changed behavior and deteriorating appearance, urged Janine to date other boys. There were lots of arguments about this, and Janine became withdrawn at home, avoiding family activities. Preoccupied with Matt's problems, Janine neglected her own responsibilities, including homework.

One day, a teacher at school reported seeing Matt sniffing cocaine in the parking lot. Matt asked Janine to cover up for him by saying that he was somewhere else with her at that time. Reluctantly, she agreed to do it. Since Janine was well liked and trusted by the faculty, they believed her, and Matt got off the hook.

But Janine grew more and more resentful about having to cover up for Matt. When she tried talking to him about that, he accused her of nagging. He even started to blame her for his getting high. "Who wouldn't," he asked, "if they had to listen to someone hassling them all the time like this?"

Janine's opinion of herself went downhill. She began to think maybe Matt *did* turn to drugs because she wasn't a good enough girlfriend. She became depressed, and when she sank very, very low she finally went to talk to a counselor at school.

At first, talking to someone she hardly knew was difficult, but soon she opened up and told the counselor everything. Janine found it actually felt good to get some of these problems out in the open.

The counselor, who was trained in substance abuse problems, knew that Janine needed certain facts. The first thing she pointed out was that Matt's problems had nothing to do with Janine. "You can't cause someone's addiction," the counselor said, "any more than you can cause them to get diabetes or some other disease!"

Next the counselor told her she also couldn't make Matt stop using drugs. Just as she hadn't caused him to turn to drugs, the counselor said, she couldn't stop him either—no

Many schools now have trained drug abuse counselors who can help students with drug-related problems.

matter *what* she did. However, covering up and bailing Matt out of trouble could actually *delay* his getting help.

The counselor suggested that Janine stop "enabling" Matt. That's what she called covering up. It's enabling the person to continue using drugs by making it easier, by eliminating the negative consequences. After all, the counselor asked, if Matt wasn't having any problems as a result of his drug use, why would he want to stop?

The other thing Janine could do, she learned, was to help *herself,* to get her own life back in order. To do this, she would first have to distance herself from Matt's problems. That meant Janine had to stop focusing her attention on him and start living her own life again—even if he never got help.

Helping Yourself

It is common to try to help a drug abuser as Janine did, by protecting him or her from getting in trouble at home, at school, or on the job. With all good intentions, many friends and relatives have lied for drug abusers, given them money, taken over responsibilities for them, or otherwise bailed them out.

If you have a friend or relative using cocaine, you may want to apply what Janine learned to yourself. There are several steps to take to help yourself.

First, you will have to detach (separate) yourself from the other person's drug problem and focus on your own behavior and your own life. This can be hard at first. You may feel as though you're being selfish and uncaring.

But remember what you are now learning about addictions: The sooner your friend or relative has to deal with the consequences of drug use, the sooner he or she will start facing the fact that it's a problem.

Second (and this may be the hardest), it will be important

to take an honest look at yourself. Are you coping in ways that are destructive to you—like using drugs yourself? Have you let things go in your life that were important to you? Have you become overinvolved in the drug user's problems as a way of avoiding your own?

Third, in order to stop focusing on the drug user's problems and build a healthy lifestyle for yourself, you will need to get involved in activities you enjoy. These might be sports, clubs, exercise, volunteer work, going to movies, reading— whatever is fun and satisfying for you. It's OK for you to have a good time—even if the abuser in your life is still having problems.

It will help to get support from others in making these changes in yourself, and there are many ways to do that. Attending a self-help group with other friends and relatives of drug abusers is one. Some schools have drug abuse counselors whom you can also talk to privately. Or try to get help from a clinic, hotline, religious leader, youth worker, or any trusted adult.

It is best to choose someone to talk to who has knowledge about drug problems, however. Because the more you continue to learn about this, the easier it will be for you to take the right steps for yourself and the drug abuser in your life.

The truth is, changing yourself is the only thing you can do. It's a big job, but an extremely important one. Evaluating your own behavior won't be easy, but it can make a major difference in your life—now and in the future.

When There Is Neglect or Abuse at Home

Suzanne's mother became verbally abusive whenever she got high on cocaine and alcohol—which was often. Suzanne would be told she was stupid, worthless, and the cause of all the family's problems. Each time, Suzanne, eighteen, would counter her mother's cruel remarks with accusations of her own. The result would be a two- or three-hour fight that left Suzanne feeling drained, guilty, and depressed.

A youth worker whom Suzanne confided in helped her learn how to protect herself. First, he said, whenever the abusive fighting started Suzanne should try to remember that her mother had the "disease" (or problem) of addiction. Remembering this, Suzanne wouldn't be as likely to take her remarks and behavior to heart.

Second, he said, it might be necessary for Suzanne to physically remove herself from each situation. Whenever Suzanne's mom started to become cruel, Suzanne was to calmly pull back from the discussion and go up to her room. If necessary, she could even leave the house and go to stay with her friend Jill.

This backup plan was arranged ahead of time, so that when the next big fight came, Suzanne quickly called Jill and left the house. Leaving her own home was a drastic step, but Suzanne did find that her own self-esteem and confidence improved each time she protected herself from these abusive attacks.

Robert had a different kind of problem. Robert's parents were both crack users, and there were times when they didn't come home all night. Once they left Robert, then eleven, and his three younger sisters alone for a whole weekend.

He remembers how they all huddled together through the night in the bedroom—scared and growing more and more hungry. His parents' drug addiction had become so severe that even caring for their children became less important to them than getting and using crack.

The next time Robert went to school, his teacher noticed that he looked very upset and asked him what was wrong. Robert stayed late that day and told her everything that had happened. Like most teachers today, she knew what to do to help.

After listening to Robert, the teacher called a social worker, who came and talked to them both. Next, the social worker made plans to meet with Robert's parents. At first, Robert felt scared about this, thinking his parents would be mad at him for talking to someone about their problem.

But the social worker was used to helping families with difficult problems. She helped Robert's parents to see that the real problem was their drug use and even enrolled them in a drug treatment program so they could begin getting help.

Even though his parents have stopped using crack, things are still not perfect at Robert's home. There are other problems too. But Robert knows now that he does not ever have to be afraid and alone, and that if anything scary happens again, he can get help.

If something like this has ever happened to you, or you fear it might, you need to get help too, and the time to do it is now. Don't wait for a crisis like Robert's to happen. Talk to a family member who doesn't use drugs, a favorite teacher, a counselor, your religious leader, or another trusted adult about what is happening or what you are afraid of.

With that trusted adult, make an emergency plan so that if you *are* ever scared, unsure of what is happening, or being neglected or abused in any way, you will know what to do. That means having a list of phone numbers you can call, including police, child protective agency, relatives, friends, whoever can help you.

Once you have a plan made and telephone numbers ready, you can feel more secure and safe. Then it makes sense to go about your life as normally as possible and not to dwell on the possibility of a problem unless one occurs.

If you are in immediate danger and don't know how to get

help, however, call the police or child protection agency. You can find these phone numbers in most phone books or by calling the operator.

Help for the Cocaine Abuser

Patti, a pretty high school senior, looks back on how she felt growing up with a mother who abused both Valium and cocaine. "I could never understand why she didn't just stop," Patti says, "especially when she could see it was hurting my father, my little brother, and me. It seemed like she just didn't care."

What Patti didn't know then is that it takes more than willpower for someone with a drug addiction to stop. It almost always takes outside help, from either a professional treatment program or a self-help group.

Remember, cocaine addiction is caused by changes the drug has made in the user's brain chemistry. It is *not* moral weakness, mental illness, or lack of love for others that is causing it. The addiction is a physical and psychological "disease."

Coming to understand this has helped Patti to feel less embarrassed about her mother's problems, too. Now she knows that having a drug problem is not the sign of a bad or crazy family; it can happen to anyone.

Patti also learned with relief that people addicted to cocaine can and do recover and lead normal lives again. But because denial of the problem is such a powerful part of it, a drug user rarely gets help until a serious crisis strikes.

The crisis could be an arrest, a cocaine-related accident or illness, or the end of a job or marriage. It usually takes a major loss for the abuser to admit there is a problem.

Hospitalization of the cocaine abuser is usually required only in severe cases, so most can be treated at an outpatient clinic. A good treatment program will provide individual, group, and family counseling, as well as education about addiction. Some counselors also teach relapse prevention techniques, specific ways to deal with the intense drug cravings and avoid using cocaine again.

The program will also require that all use of cocaine be stopped immediately upon entering treatment. In fact, the only way to successfully overcome an addiction is to stop using cocaine and all other drugs completely.

This is very difficult for most drug abusers to face at first, but treatment centers and self-help groups can provide the support and help to make it possible.

Group counseling is usually an important part of treatment for cocaine addiction.

Self-help groups such as Cocaine Anonymous and Narcotics Anonymous are helping a lot of people recover from cocaine addiction, too. In fact, those who go to a professional treatment program will probably also need to attend a self-help group several times a week in the early stages of recovery.

Remember, cocaine addiction is a chronic problem. That means it can recur. Sometimes a person comes into treatment for a while, then lapses back into using cocaine. That person may have to experience more problems resulting from cocaine use before truly facing the problem and becoming committed to stopping.

8

Prevention

The National Debate

With the number of cocaine users still climbing and the availability of an even more deadly form—crack—many of our politicians, drug abuse experts, and police are searching for ways to stem the epidemic.

One approach has been to try to slow cocaine production in South America. To this end, the U.S. Army joined Bolivian police to raid coca processing labs there in 1986. But while eighteen centers were destroyed, cocaine production was only slowed down for a short time. What's worse, new labs sprang up elsewhere in South America.

In an effort to reduce coca crops, the U.S. government recently offered to pay $140 per acre to Bolivian farmers who destroyed their plants. Very few were willing to do this, however, since an acre of coca is worth the much higher price of $2,000 when sold for cocaine.

Efforts are always being made to stop cocaine from being brought into the United States, but this is no small task, either. Cocaine is easy to hide because it is so compact, and smugglers, eager for the enormous profits it brings, keep finding new ways to sneak it in.

Even though drug enforcement officials are seizing ten times more cocaine coming into the United States than they were just five years ago, the supply of cocaine in the streets remains greater than ever.

This is just one of the many cocaine processing labs in Bolivia.

A third way to reduce the supply of cocaine is to get tough on dealers. This means stepping up local police efforts, as New York did when it formed a special crack unit. But there are problems with this approach, too: The more time police spend on drug investigations, the less they have to fight other crime.

There has been talk of relaxing the laws governing police "search and seizure" and wiretapping procedures in order to aid drug invesgitations. Critics of these proposed changes, however, warn that in our fervor to stop drug crime, we could threaten the very foundation of our free society.

It is doubtful anyway, these critics say, that cocaine use *can* be eliminated by law enforcement. In the 1920s, when alcohol was illegal here (a period known as Prohibition), many people continued to make and use alcoholic beverages despite the efforts of police.

Still another approach that's been suggested is to reduce cocaine use by identifying and penalizing users. More and more employers are requiring applicants and current workers to submit urine samples for drug screening. In 1986 President Reagan, in a controversial move, ordered the drug testing of all federal employees.

There are serious questions about the legality of such drug screens, though. In at least thirteen cases so far, judges have ruled that they violate Fourth Amendment protections in our Constitution against unreasonable search and seizure. The tests are also unreliable, since a number come back "positive" even when no drugs have been used.

As long as there is a demand for cocaine from American drug consumers, it seems, there will be someone with cocaine to sell. Police and drug enforcement efforts alone are not likely to stop the epidemic, and cutting back on our valued civil rights seems a dangerous road to go down.

The more basic problem to address, perhaps, is not the availability of cocaine and crack, but the fact that so many Americans are willing to try these and other drugs.

Changing Attitudes

Nearly 37 million Americans (one out of every five people over age twelve) used one or more illegal drugs in the last year! That astounding statistic tells us clearly that drugs of all sorts have become deeply ingrained in American life.

But using drugs doesn't *have* to be accepted as normal, as "just part of growing up." We could see the widespread drug use around us now as a sign that our society is in very deep trouble.

It's a sign that many people are trying to escape from their problems rather than find ways to resolve them, and that changes in our family life and communities have resulted in the neglect of some of our emotional needs.

It's also a sign that pressure to perform and achieve in school and in our careers has blinded us to the things in life that really matter. We have been robbed of true feelings of self-worth in favor of maintaining an image.

These are the things we need to work on to make our society a better, more supportive place to live. But first, we have to make sure we stay drug-free so we can do it. What that means, ultimately, is that our attitudes toward drug use must change.

The message that drug abuse is unacceptable, unhealthy, and unnecessary must be communicated by all of us who care about ourselves and our nation. And being drug-free must become as desirable a personal trait as being physically fit and attractive. What we have to come to realize is that using drugs doesn't help a person succeed but becomes instead a major obstacle.

For evidence that a shift in public attitude *can* make a difference, we need only look at two other health and safety threats that have been reduced: cigarette smoking and drunk driving. The number of deaths from each of these has decreased as more and more people have joined in public disapproval of the behaviors.

Fortunately, attitudes toward illegal drugs are already starting to change. The use of all drugs except cocaine has either remained steady or gone down in the past three years. (Unfortunately, that still leaves America with more drug use than any other industrialized nation.)

Changing our national attitude toward drugs is a big job but not an impossible one. It's an effort that all segments of society must become involved in, not just a few. We will need the cooperation of schools, the media, businesses, health professionals, legal experts, politicians, parents, students, athletes, celebrities—and you.

What You Can Do

The best way to avoid being one of the people who develop a problem with cocaine or crack is not to try these drugs. It's as simple as that. By even trying them you enter the risk group from which some will go on to become dependent or suffer other harm.

Of those who try cocaine powder, for instance, one-fifth are thought to become dependent on it. Of those who try crack, at least one-third get trapped. But of those who never try either of these drugs, *none* go on to be harmed by them!

Since there is no way to predict *who* will be among the percentage that will get addicted or (beyond that) become paranoid, or have a panic attack, or suffer brain seizures, or even die—why take the risk?

One way to avoid being tempted to try drugs like cocaine

81

is to stay away from "gateway" drugs like tobacco, alcohol, and marijuana. For it's a fact that once a person begins taking a casual attitude toward these drugs, he or she becomes more likely to try cocaine and other more harmful ones, too. Of those who have smoked marijuana 100 times or more, statistics show, a full 12 percent are currently using cocaine.

But how *can* you avoid trying cocaine or crack when it is around you and when it is offered? By learning certain simple communication skills and having the courage to apply them when the time comes.

Saying "No"

In recent years, nationwide advertising campaigns aimed at reducing teenage drug use have urged young people to "just say no" to drugs. Of course, it's not so easy for any of us— young or old—to just say "no" to something when we feel

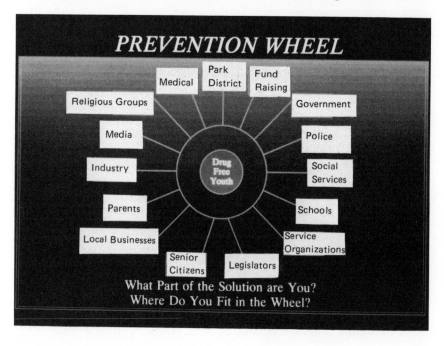

under pressure from others to conform. It's the same pressure that makes us give in and buy something we don't want to buy, or lend something we don't want to lend.

It's common to want to be included in what others are doing and to avoid appearing different or left out. But the important thing here is to learn to differentiate between the things worth taking a stand on and the things we can let go by.

For instance, if you give in to someone's suggestion that you buy a certain item of clothing that's in fashion, the worst that can happen is that you buy something you really don't like or feel comfortable in. It would be ideal to be able to say "no" even to this, or to anything you do not freely choose yourself.

But if you give in to someone's suggestion that you try cocaine or crack, the price you pay for giving in is likely to be a lot steeper, possibly even life-threatening. So those are the kinds of decisions to concentrate on first.

Sometimes the pressure to try a drug doesn't come from other people but from inside of us. We may pressure ourselves to try something in order to fit in or at least not stand out as someone who is "different" or "scared."

When we are pressuring ourselves, it helps to talk to someone like a supportive friend, parent, teacher, or counselor who can help us get things back in perspective. Sometimes all we need is to be reminded that we are OK just the way we are—drug-free—and that we don't have to prove anything to anyone else!

There are specific communication techniques you can learn to help you say "no" to drugs—or to anything you don't want. Sometimes this is called assertiveness. What it consists of, basically, is learning to say "no" simply and firmly—without making excuses or defending your decision in any way.

You don't have to get mad at the other person, either. In fact, it's better if you don't. You can simply remain calm and friendly—and say "no" in whatever way is most comfortable for you:

"No, thanks."

"No, that's OK."

"I'll pass."

"I'm OK."

"I don't want any, thanks."

"No."

But just saying "no" to what you *don't* want (in this case, drugs) is not usually enough, either. The next step is to begin to say "yes" to all the positive things you *do* want in your life—to play a sport or a musical instrument; to succeed in school or help others through volunteer work; or to do something creative, like paint or draw a picture.

Do things that are just plain *fun* too, whether that's going to movies, skiing, swimming, reading, or sitting around laughing with your friends—those deep-down belly laughs that feel so good.

An eighty-five-year-old Kentucky woman, Nadine Starr, once wrote that if she could live her life over she would "climb more mountains, swim more rivers, eat more ice cream, start barefoot earlier in spring, go to more dances, ride more merry-go-rounds, and pick more daisies." Most of us could benefit from her advice!

One Last Word

The real difference in the cocaine epidemic in America will be made by *you*. What you decide to do, how you respond to other people's drug use, the attitudes you express, and the example you set have the power to influence others.

You can't control what other people do, it's true. But you can let it be known where you stand on drugs. And just by not using them yourself you'll be making a powerful statement to those around you.

You'll be saying that you choose not to escape from reality, but to work to make it better; not to become sickly and unattractive, but to look and feel the best that you can; not to resign yourself to failure, but to give yourself every shot at success. In short, by deciding not to take a chance with cocaine, crack, and other drugs, you'll be choosing a better life.

For Further Information

The American Council for Drug
   Educ.
204 Monroe St.
Rockville, Md. 20850
(301) 294-0600

Free catalog of materials.

Cocaine Anonymous
World Service Office
P. O. Box 1367
Culver City, Ca. 90239
(213) 559-5800

*Free help for cocaine abusers.
Call or write for nearest meeting
locations.*

Cocanon Family Groups
East Coast Office
P. O. Box 1080—Cooper
   Station
New York, N.Y. 10276 – 1080
Eastern U.S. Hotline:
(212) 713-5133

*Free help for families and friends
of cocaine abusers. Call or write
for nearest meeting locations.*

Cocanon Family Groups
West Coast Office
P. O. Box 3969
Hollywood, Ca. 90028
Western U.S. Hotline:
(213) 859-2206

*Free help for families and friends
of cocaine abusers. Call or write
for nearest meeting locations.*

Drug Referral Hotline
(800) 622-HELP *(no charge)*

*Free and confidential referral to
drug treatment programs.
Operated by National Institute
on Drug Abuse*

Hale House Center
68 Edgecomb Ave.
New York, N.Y. 10030
(212) 690-5623

*Help for babies and children of
drug-addicted parents.*

Hazelden Educational Materials
Box 176
Center City, Minn. 55012
(800) 328-9000 *(no charge)*

*Free catalog of books and
pamphlets on various drug
problems.*

Narcotics Education, Inc.
6830 Laurel St.
Washington D.C. 20012 – 9979
(800) 548-8700 *(no charge)*

Free catalog

The Washton Institute
Outpatient Addiction
   Treatment Centers
4 Park Ave.
New York, N.Y. 10016
(212) 213-4900
                also
933 Saw Mill River Rd.
Ardsley, N.Y. 10502
(914) 693-1010

*Treatment for cocaine, alcohol,
and other drug addictions.*

Narcotics Anonymous
World Service Office
P. O. Box 9999
Van Nuys, Ca. 91409
(818) 780-3951

*Free help for all narcotics users.
Call or write for nearest meeting
locations.*

National Clearinghouse on Drug
   Abuse Information
P. O. Box 416
Kensington, MD. 20795
(301) 443-6500

Free materials

P.R.I.D.E.
Woodruff Bldg., Suite 1002
100 Edgewood Ave.
Atlanta, Ga. 30303
(800) 241-9746 *(no charge)*

*Resource and information center.
Publishes youth group handbook
and other publications.*

Glossary

addiction—A condition marked by the repeated, uncontrolled use of a drug despite harmful consequences.

addictive—Capable of causing addiction. Cocaine is addictive.

amphetamine—A drug that stimulates the central nervous system, increasing heart rate and blood pressure. Also known as speed.

anesthetic—A drug that produces temporary insensitivity to pain.

brain seizure—A malfunction of electrical charges in the brain, often resulting in violent, involuntary muscle jerks and loss of consciousness. Can also cause heart, lungs or other organs to stop.

bust—Slang for police arrest.

cardiac arrest—A sudden stoppage of the heart.

coca paste—A pasty substance extracted from coca leaves and smoked, much like crack. Coca paste, known as "basuco," may cause permanent lung and brain damage.

cocaine—Cocaine hydrochloride, a powerfully addictive local anesthetic and central nervous system stimulant extracted from coca leaves.

cocaine psychosis—A mental condition usually resulting from repeated cocaine use, marked by hallucinations, delusions, and paranoia.

crack—The street name for preprocessed cocaine freebase, a smokable form of cocaine that's sold in tiny "rocks" or tablets.

crack houses—Buildings or apartments where crack is secretly sold and used.

crash—A condition following a cocaine high, caused by a depletion of dopamine in the brain, and marked by depression, tiredness, irritability, and cravings for more cocaine.

cuts—Chemicals added to cocaine by dealers in order to increase its volume and weight and therefore bring in more profit.

delusion—A false belief. Heavy cocaine users often develop paranoid delusions, a persistent false belief that someone is pursuing them or seeking to do them harm.

depression—An emotional state marked by chronic feelings of sadness and hopelessness.

dopamine—A brain chemical (neurotransmitter) essential to normal nerve activity in the brain. Cocaine use alters dopamine levels.

dopamine depletion—A condition caused by repeated cocaine use wherin brain nerve cells lack sufficient dopamine to maintain a normal mood state.

drug screening—Testing of a urine or blood sample to detect any drugs recently used.

enabling—An act that enables, or helps, a drug user to continue using without facing the consequences. Covering up, for example, is enabling.

epidemic—A disease or condition affecting many people.

Erythroxylon coca—The coca plant, from which cocaine is made.

freebase—The cocaine "base" which is left when hydrochloride is removed by heating. *Freebasing* refers to the act of smoking cocaine freebase.

gateway drugs—Drugs such as tobacco, alcohol, and marijuana which often serve as a "gateway" or introduction into other drug use.

hallucinate—To see or hear something that is not really there.

heart attack—A malfunction of the heart caused by reduced or blocked blood flow to the heart muscle. Also known as a coronary.

heroin—An addictive narcotic drug derived from the poppy plant.

high—Euphoric effects of a drug. With cocaine, the high is caused by the stimulant effects and by the release of dopamine in the brain.

high blood pressure—A condition that results when blood exerts abnormal pressure against walls of blood vessels. Also known as hypertension.

hypothalamus—The part of the brain housing the reward center, where cocaine addiction is thought to occur.

insomnia—Inability to sleep normally.

intravenous—A method of drug use by which the substance, in liquid form, is injected into a vein.

kindling effect—The increased ability of a drug, after repeated use, to cause overstimulation of the brain. With cocaine, the kindling effect can prompt brain seizures.

methamphetamine—A drug that stimulates the central nervous system, increasing heart rate and blood pressure. Also known as speed.

marijuana—A drug derived from the hemp plant, usually smoked in joints, or cigarettes.

narcotic—A drug that causes drowsiness and relief of pain; most classified narcotics (excluding cocaine) are opiates, made from poppy flowers.

neuron—A nerve cell that conducts nerve impulses.

neurotransmitter—A substance that transmits nerve impulses from one neuron to the next.

opium—An addictive narcotic drug made from the poppy flower.

overdose—Any dose of a drug that causes a toxic (adverse) reaction.

panic attack—A temporary mental condition marked by extreme and unreasoning fear and anxiety.

paranoia—A mental condition marked by fear and extreme suspiciousness of others.

receptor site—An area on a neuron which receives specific neurotransmitters, such as dopamine.

recovery—The act of getting well. Recovery from cocaine addiction is usually a lifelong process.

relapse prevention techniques—Specific methods that can be used to counter drug cravings and avoid further drug use.

reuptake process—Process by which excess dopamine is normally carried back to the nerve cell that released it. Cocaine interferes with this process.

reward center—A part of the brain, located in the hypothalamus, where basic biological drives are reinforced and where cocaine cravings are thought to be set in motion by repeated cocaine use.

rock—A street name for crack.

schizophrenia—A form of mental illness, a psychosis, marked by a loss of contact with reality, often accompanied by hallucinations, delusions, and paranoia.

self-help group—An informal, nonprofessional group formed to help people overcome a specific problem. These groups are usually free and confidential, as are Cocaine Anonymous and Narcotics Anonymous.

speedball—A mixture of cocaine and heroin.

stimulant—A drug that speeds up the central nervous system.

stroke—Sudden paralysis or loss of sensation resulting from damaged brain tissue, usually caused by a burst blood vessel in the brain.

synapse—The space between neurons, where nerve impulses are transmitted.

tolerance—Reduced sensitivity to a drug's high, requiring a higher dose to achieve the same effects.

toxic reaction—An adverse physical or psychiatric reaction to a drug.

vasoconstrictor—A substance that causes blood vessels to constrict, or narrow.

vesicles—Microscopic structures on a neuron where dopamine is stored.

withdrawal symptoms—Unpleasant physical or psychological effects that occur when an addictive drug is stopped.

Further Reading

BOOKS

Allen, David F., ed. *The Cocaine Crisis*. New York: Plenum Books, 1987.

Britt, David. *The All American Cocaine Story*. Minneapolis, Minn: Compcare, 1984.

Brown, David. *Crack and Cocaine*. New York: Franklin Watts, 1987.

Chatlos, Calvin. *Crack: What You Should Know About the Cocaine Epidemic*. New York: Putnam, 1987.

Frazer, Loraine. *Cocaine and Crack*. New York: Franklin Watts, 1987.

Hyde, Margaret O. *Addictions*. New York: McGraw-Hill, 1987.

Johanson, Chris-Ellyn. *Cocaine: A New Epidemic*. New York: Chelsea House, 1986.

Stone, Nannette, et al., *Cocaine: Seduction and Solution*. New York: Pinnacle Books, 1984.

Woods, Geraldine and Harold Woods. *Cocaine*. New York: Franklin Watts, 1985.

PERIODICALS

"Can Cocaine Conquer America?" *Reader's Digest,* January 1987, pp. 30–37.

"Cocaine: Could You Get Hooked?" *New Woman,* June 1986, pp. 62–64.

"Coke: The Random Killer." *Discover,* March 1985, pp. 17–22.

"Coping With Cocaine." *The Atlantic Monthly,* January 1986, pp. 39–47.

"Crack" *Time,* June 2, 1986, pp. 16–18.

"Crack and Crime." *Newsweek,* June 16, 1986, pp. 16–22.

"Crack: The Road Back." *Newsweek,* June 30, 1986, pp. 52–53.

"Fighting Cocaine's Grip: Millions of Users, Billions of Dollars." *Time,* April 11, 1983, pp. 22–27.

"Kids and Cocaine." *Newsweek,* June 30, 1986, pp. 58–65.

"Saying No." *Newsweek,* August 11, 1986, pp. 14–16.

Index

362.2
Was

Washton, Arnold M.
Cocaine and crack :
what you need to know

DATE DUE			
JUN 6			
FEB 2 4 1995			
APR 8 1995			
MAY 3 0 1996			
NOV 2 6 1997			
JAN 2 9 1998			
MAY 0 8 1998			
JUN 2 8 '01			
MAY 3 1 2007			